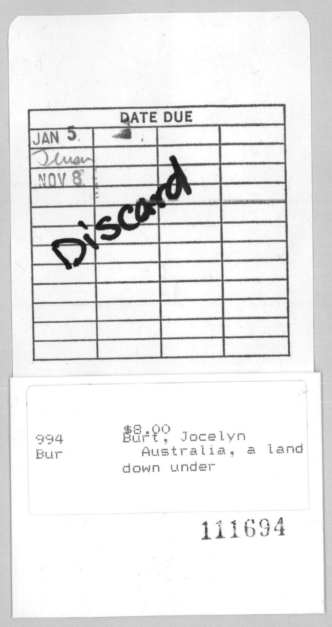

Jocelyn Burt's

AUSTRALIA

A LAND DOWN UNDER

Jocelyn Burt's
AUSTRALIA
A LAND DOWN UNDER

The Five Mile Press

The Five Mile Press
20 Liddiard Street,
Hawthorn, Victoria 3122 Australia

First published 1984
Reprinted 1986

Designed by Derrick I. Stone Design
Typesetting by Meredith Trade Lino, Melbourne
Printed in Hong Kong by Dai Nippon Printing Company Ltd.

National Library of Australia
Cataloguing-in-Publication Data.

Burt, Jocelyn.
    Australia, a land down under.
    ISBN 0 86788 056 2.

    1. Australia — description and travel — 1976 — views.
    I. Title
919.4'0463.

Cover
THE OLGAS.

Frontispiece
WINDMILL, NEAR HOLBROOK. One of the most
common sights throughout rural and outback
Australia is the windmill, which pumps
precious water from the artesian basin for
livestock, and for use on farms, irrigated areas,
domestic and town supplies. It has been
estimated that well over a quarter of a million
windmills dot the countryside.

CONTENTS

CANBERRA. Australia's capital city, Canberra lies in the Australian Capital Territory which was created in 1908, and covers 2356 square kilometres near Goulburn in New South Wales.

This is Lake Burley Griffin, with the High Court visible through the misty curtain of the Waterjet.

ACKNOWLEDGEMENTS

I would like to thank Doug Fearon of Austrek Safaris, Cairns, for assistance in the Gulf Country; the National Parks and Wildlife Service in New South Wales; and Dick Lang of Desert-Trek Australia. Photo credit: Page 33 Great Barrier Reef, off Heron Island: Valerie Taylor/Australasian Nature Transparencies; Page 58 Perth, from Kings Park: Richard Woldendorp/Photographic Library of Australia.

THE TWELVE APOSTLES, PORT CAMPBELL. These unusual stacks rearing over the powerful surf are just some of many fascinating landforms that are in the Port Campbell National Park, which covers about 32 kilometres of coastline between Cape Otway and Warrnambool in western Victoria. This is a treacherous stretch of coast for shipping, and in the past has claimed over fifty vessels and many lives.

INTRODUCTION

An unprecedented number of people from all over the world are now discovering that Australia is a land of extremes and unique beauty. Australians have long been aware of their country's individual character and many thousands make the most of weekends, holidays and retirement to explore its marvellous scenery and fascinating wildlife and wildflowers. Many places of interest lie relatively close to cities and towns, but travellers must cover great distances to reach the beauty of the vast wilderness areas.

Although Australia is the world's smallest continent, many motorists only discover its great size by attempting to travel around the country. Its land area is roughly equal to the United States (not including Alaska). The mainland stretches 3200 kilometres from the most northerly point at Cape York to Wilsons Promontory in the south. The distance from west to east — Streep Point near Dirk Hartog Island to Cape Byron — measures about 4000 kilometres. Yet this great area has a population of only 15 million with settlement confined mainly to the fertile eastern and south-eastern regions.

Australia is also the flattest and oldest of the world's continents. Some of its land surfaces have been continuously exposed above sea level for around 1500 million years, and geologists have discovered rocks that are twice that age. The geological forces that formed much of the earth into high mountain ranges during the last 100 million years did not affect Australia. As a result, its surface has had time to settle down and has been worn and sculpted only by the elements. Its antiquity shows, especially when it is seen from the air during a drought, with every ridge, dune and plain laid bare.

Australia is the driest separate land mass on earth. Many areas have an extremely erratic rainfall and floods tend to follow droughts as night follows day. There is also enormous evaporation from its lakes and rivers: the total run-off of water to the ocean, including that from the Murray-Darling, its only large river system, is less than that of the Mississippi in the United States. The great watershed for nearly half of Australia — and its only continental mountain chain — is the forested Great Dividing Range in the east, which stretches from Cape York in the north to western Victoria in the south. Parts of the range even reach into the island State of Tasmania. This important backbone of Australia gives rise on its eastern side to a multitude of streams and rivers that nourish the fertile land. To the west, the watercourses spill far out to the thirsty, arid plains and in many cases eventually disappear into sandy deserts or salt lakes.

Mountains are generally held to be places of great beauty, and the Great Dividing Range is no exception. Much of Australia's loveliest scenery lies in its foothills, and in its countless spectacular cliffs and gorges, bold bluffs and wild peaks, high plains and mountain lakes. What many Australians call mountains would seem to be little more than hills to Europeans and Americans; but Australia does have the Australian Alps, whose highest peak, the craggy, boulder-studded Mount Kosciusko, reaches to 2330 metres. Much of the Great Dividing Range is wild country, virtually inaccessible. During winter, many of the peaks and plateaux in southern New South Wales, Victoria, and Tasmania are blanketed in snow, while to the north, tropical sunlight filters through lush rainforests that clothe many steep slopes and high peaks.

Throughout the rest of the continent, numerous ranges give birth to lesser rivers and streams. For south-western Australia the most important river system is the Swan-Avon, which rises on the Darling Plateau and empties into the Indian Ocean, at Perth. In the north, many rivers are fed by monsoonal rains that fall only between December and April. At such times they become colossal, fast-flowing watercourses that flood widely over the plains to *fill lagoons and billabongs before pouring wastefully into the sea. Then, as the harsh 'Dry' season sets in, these swollen streams gradually diminish in volume until, by November, they may again be nothing more than a string of pools waiting to be replenished.*

The western half of the continent has no mountains to equal those of the Great Dividing Range, and so this section of the country — particularly central Australia — has a much lower rainfall. However, it is in these arid regions that some of Australia's most spectacular beauty can be found. The 'outback' as it is known, generally includes all the land that lies well beyond the coastal cities, towns and settled rural areas. It totals about three-quarters of the continent.

There are six major Australian deserts: the Great Sandy, the Gibson, the Great Victoria, the Tanami, the Simpson, and Sturt's Stony Desert. Although these areas are cruel wastes where plains of glittering gibber stones give way to vivid red sand-dunes, low-lying rock-studded ranges, and great stretches of domed, prickly spinifex, they possess an extraordinary beauty. Most of the lakes are dry, thickly encrusted with glistening salt, while the rivers are mere beds of sand, flowing only after the occasional good rain. Travellers venturing into these areas must be well-equipped and have suitable four-wheel-drive vehicles. Even in recent years, lives have been claimed by these deserts — although when such tragedies do occur, it is usually because travellers have not taken the necessary precautions, or have not heeded warnings by local inhabitants.

Some of Australia's most famous scenery lies in the heart of the continent, drawing tourists from everywhere. Rugged ranges, many of them slashed with magnificent chasms, gaps, and gorges, display astonishing beauty and colour which change during the day, as they respond to the capricious variations of directional light. Sometimes the superb effect is increased by the presence of pools of still water lying in the gorges, reflecting craggy walls, or where water spreads along the normally dry rivers that carve their way through colourful sand country. Equally colourful are the strange monoliths that rise dramatically from the plains — the most well-known being Ayers Rock, the Olgas, and Chambers Pillar.

The heart of the continent may be renowned for its unique and colourful beauty, but Australia's 38 000-kilometre coastline provides just as much diverse and fascinating scenery. A good deal of the coast, particularly in the north and north-west, is wild country, where access is sometimes made almost impossible either by mud flats and thick forests of mangroves which present a daunting barrier on land, or by treacherous reefs and unpredictable currents and tides which make a seaward approach hazardous. To the south and east, coastal plains and mountains may end abruptly at rock-encrusted shores or sheer off into spectacular, sometimes terrifyingly steep cliffs. A good portion of the Great Australian Bight is bound by the longest line of unbroken cliffs in the world, plunging in places to 130 metres. There are many remarkable landforms. Some of them, such as those near Port Campbell in Victoria and at Eaglehawk Neck in Tasmania are boldly prominent, while others conceal their weird or grand formations in caves and rugged terrain.

Much of the coast is washed by surf, and what a thrilling sight it is to see the long rolling waves, capped with plumes of flying white spray, break against the rocks or over sand. But there are just as many quiet spots, where streams spread into lagoons sheltering behind barriers of sand, or where rivers flow into quiet inlets and widen out to estuaries before emptying into the sea. A large section of the Queensland coast is relatively sheltered by the Great Barrier Reef, the massive and fantastic wall of coral that runs for 2000 kilometres from the Torres Strait to just south of the Tropic of Capricorn.

Best-loved of all the coastal areas are the beaches, which are among the world's finest.

SNOWY RIVER, NEAR WILLIS. For most of its course from the slopes of Mount Kosciusko in the Snowy Mountains, to its mouth at Marlo near Orbost, the Snowy River flows through wild and rugged terrain, much of which is inaccessible except to the white water canoeists. Close to the New South Wales border, the river runs by the road, and in summer, when the water level is very low, it is possible to walk a considerable way along this beautiful river.

Some of them sweep unbroken to distant horizons, earning such names as the Eighty Mile Beach or the Ninety Mile Beach, while others are small, fitting snugly into coves and inlets. Their sand varies in colour from pure white, through all the shades of gold and light brown to red. Rarely is it coarse, and in parts of south-west Western Australia it is so fine that it squeaks underfoot, and when pressed in the hands resembles talcum powder.

Australians make the most of their beaches, and water sports such as surfing, board-riding, yachting, and swimming are immensely popular. Beach activities are not restricted to the warmer months, and all year round enthusiastic walkers and joggers enjoy a brisk tramp or trot along the water's edge, breathing in the invigorating ozone-filled air. Even board-riders put on wetsuits and brave the winter elements in order to catch good breakers. Away from the more densely-populated city beaches, it is usually possible to find a quiet and secluded spot, and feel the place is yours. Not surprisingly, many Australians believe that their beaches epitomise the essential freedom that this country offers so widely.

SHOWY BANKSIA *(Banksia speciosa)*. This spectacular species of banksia is only found in the sandy heaths of the Eyre district, extending from Hopetoun to Israelite Bay in southern Western Australia. There are about 58 species of *Banksia* in Australia — and 46 of these are from the West.

NEW SOUTH WALES

The most populated and oldest of the Australian States, New South Wales occupies an area of 801,428 square kilometres and has a population in excess of 5.25 million.

The name New South Wales was applied to eastern Australia by James Cook during his voyages of 1770. Eight years later, Governor Arthur Phillip and the First Fleet arrived at Sydney Cove to establish a colony which served primarily as a dumping ground for Britain's unwanted criminals. Initially confined to the coastal area, the colony eventually began to move inland once a way was found through the Blue Mountains in 1813. Free settlers and convicts who had served out their time, were quick to establish extensive farming and grazing properties and for many years the prosperity of New South Wales rode on the sheeps' back. The State is still Australia's most productive farming area but it has also developed significant mining and manufacturing industries.

The capital, Sydney, is one of the world's great modern cities, with a population of more than three million who enjoy a magnificent harbour and some of the Pacific's most spectacular surf beaches. For visitors there are endless attractions — the world famous Harbour Bridge, the controversial Opera House, the historic Rocks area, theatres, licensed clubs, parks, family beaches and superb waterways.

Further afield are the grand vistas of the Blue Mountains, the nearby Jenolan Caves and, in the south east, the Snowy Mountains which boast the largest engineering project ever carried out in Australia, the Snowy Mountains Irrigation and Power Generating Scheme.

The Australian Alps, snow-covered in winter, contain some excellent skiing areas as well as the country's highest mountain, Mount Kosciusko.

SYDNEY HARBOUR. At Mrs. Macquarie's Point there are superb views of the Sydney Harbour Bridge and Opera House. From this point a walking path passes through the Botanic Gardens to the Opera House. Sydney is Australia's oldest and largest city, situated around one of the world's most beautiful harbours.

1

2

3

1 MARTIN PLACE, SYDNEY. In the heart of the city, Martin Place is now a paved mall, where pedestrians can sit, or stroll among the trees, and enjoy eating outside at the numerous fine restaurants and cafes neaby. In the warmer months, it is a popular venue for lunchtime concerts.

2 WAX-LIP ORCHID (*Glossodia major*). Sometimes known as Parson-in-the-pulpit, this commonly seen orchid grows in lightly timbered and scrub country in the south eastern States, including southern Queensland. Flowering time is August to November.

3 EASTERN GREY KANGAROO. This marsupial belongs to the Macropodidae family — appropriately meaning 'great footed', of which there are over fifty species, including the wallabies, rat and tree kangaroos. Eastern Greys range from Cape York to South Australia, and it is unfortunate that their preference for good grazing country often brings them in to conflict with farmers.

4 ILLAWARRA ESCARPMENT, NEAR MOSS VALE. Situated in the Great Dividing Range, this sheer cliff face lines the Yarrunga Valley in the Morton National Park, and can be seen from the top of the Fitzroy Falls. There are walking tracks along the escarpment, and into the valley. Parking facilities for access to the national park lie close to the Moss Vale-Nowra road.

1

1 SUNSET, LAKE MENINDEE. Lying in the Kinchega National Park, 100 kilometres east of Broken Hill, Lake Menindee is the largest of a number of lakes fed by the Darling River. Since the river was dammed here, the waters have spread widely over the plains, and as a result many trees have died.

2 HAWKESBURY RIVER AT WISEMANS FERRY. The small settlement of Wisemans Ferry, 66 kilometres from Sydney, is a popular recreational ground for water sports enthusiasts. Two vehicular ferries provide regular transport across this very beautiful section of the river.

1

2

1 MURRUMBIDGEE RIVER, GUNDAGAI. When the river is low, it is possible for stock to wander from the spacious river flats in the town, known as the North Common, to the river bed itself. The Murrumbidgee is the second longest river after the Darling in New South Wales. It rises near Kiandra in the Snowy Mountains, and joins the Murray River downstream from Balranald.

2 ALPINE MINT BUSH (*Prostanthera cuneata*). This plant inhabits the alps of New South Wales, eastern Victoria, and Tasmania, and flowers between November and February.

3 RIVER GUMS, DARLING RIVER. Near Wentworth on the border, the Darling River is lined with very old, large gums. Like the Murray River, the Darling played an important role in the riverboat era, and many a paddle steamer loaded with goods passed this point. Prior to the damming of the Darling at Menindee, boats all too frequently became stranded on mud banks when the river dried out during dry seasons.

1

1 THE PINNACLES, BEN BOYD NATIONAL PARK.
Known as the Quoraburagun Pinnacles, this
stunningly colourful weathered sandstone cliff
lies back from South Long Beach in the
northern section of Ben Boyd National Park,
near Eden, on the South Coast. The cliff can be
viewed from the walking track which starts at
the parking area and loops around the cliff
tops, or from the nearby beach, where it is
possible to walk into a small valley which
contains the Pinnacles.

2 MANLY BEACH, SYDNEY. This is one of many
beaches that line the city's coastal suburbs. A
harbour ferry service from the central city to
Manly provides easy — and delightful —
access to this popular and attractive Sydney
suburb.

3 TERRIGAL. Lying on the northern outskirts of
Greater Sydney, 95 kilometres from the city,
Terrigal is one of many attractive towns that
spread along the cliff tops of this region. From
a number of vantage points along the roads,
there are superb views of rugged headlands,
rocky platforms and long beaches of golden
sand.

2

VICTORIA

Victoria is Australia's smallest mainland State, covering only three per cent of the country's total land mass. Yet within its borders lie a bewildering variety of scenery and attractions.

Melbourne, the capital, was founded in 1835 as a free settlement. Two decades later, as a result of the gold rush, the small village was transformed into a thriving city. Since then, Melbourne has developed in a gracious and dignified manner with a subtle charm that is not experienced elsewhere in the country. Its three million residents enjoy some of the finest shops, restaurants, theatres, parks and gardens to be found anywhere in the country. As an added bonus, most of the State's attractions are located less than a day's drive away.

From the rugged grandeur of the Victorian Alps to the shimmering heat of the Mallee wheatfields, Victoria has something for everyone. Magnificent vistas abound in the Grampians, along the picturesque Great Ocean Road, through Gippsland and in the Great Dividing Range. During the ski season, Victoria offers a variety of first class resorts in superb mountain scenery. In contrast to the snow, the State's coastline has many spectacular surfing beaches and hundreds of safe family swimming areas.

Inland, there are lakes for fishing and boating. For the water enthusiast, there is one of the world's greatest inland coastal lagoon systems, stretching for many kilometres from Lakes Entrance in Gippsland. More than a third of Australia's national parks are located in Victoria. They offer an unparalleled choice of scenery, flora and fauna for the enjoyment of tourists, bushwalkers and photographers.

1

1 BOTANIC GARDENS, MELBOURNE. These beautiful gardens lying close to the central city in South Yarra, are indeed a haven for Melburnians. A major feature is the birdlife, and an hour can easily be spent feeding the swans and ducks — or watching other people feed them. These gardens were the first of Melbourne's parklands to be surveyed and planted by La Trobe, in 1845.

2 WOMBARGO RANGE, EAST GIPPSLAND. Some of the finest stands of Snow Gum in Victoria are found in this range and nearby Mount Cobberas, lying in the east of the State. The road over the Wombargo Range is narrow — and lonely — and runs up to 1420 metres above sea level, consequently the range is often enveloped in cloud, which gives an eerie, but beautiful atmosphere to the forest. The eastern end of the road is only suitable for conventional vehicles in good weather.

1

2

1 RED FLOWERING GUM (*Eucalyptus ficifolia*). Although this eucalypt is a native of Western Australia, it has been cultivated widely throughout the country along roads, highways, parks and gardens.

2 KOOKABURRA. One of the best-loved birds in Australia, the Kookaburra's ringing, cheerful laugh is often heard in the bush or outer suburban areas at dawn and dusk. It is the largest of the country's ten species of kingfishers. Although its true home is eastern Australia, around the turn of the century it was introduced to Western Australia and later to Tasmania.

3 SNOW GUM, FALLS CREEK. In winter the Bogong High Plains around Falls Creek are transformed into a wonderful white world of exquisite beauty, where snow gums bend under their heavy burdens of snow, and icicles glitter on twigs, leaves and marker poles. The ski resort at Falls Creek offers some of the best skiing in the country — both for downhill and cross-country skiing.

4 MOUNT FEATHERTOP, FROM MOUNT HOTHAM. In January, there are always good displays of alpine wildflowers near the Mount Loch car park.

1

1 SORRENTO, MORNINGTON PENINSULA. Yachting is an ideal water sport for Port Phillip Bay, and most of the bay's holiday resorts have an active yacht club. The Mornington Peninsula lies immediately south east of Melbourne and separates Port Phillip Bay from Westernport.

2 SEALERS COVE, WILSONS PROMONTORY. This is at the boulders lookout, by the steep Refuge Cove track. An important national park situated in Gippsland, 225 kilometres south east of Melbourne, Wilsons Promontory is the most southerly point of the Australian mainland.

3 LORNE. This popular beach lies by the scenic Great Ocean Road, west of Geelong and 143 kilometres from Melbourne.

1

2

3

1 GOLDEN EVERLASTINGS (*Helichrysum viscosum*).This particular everlasting is found in dry forests, mainly at low altitudes, and flowers in summer.

2 YACCA — AN AUSTRALIAN GRASS TREE (*Xanthorrhoea minor*). This species of grass tree is widespread throughout Australia. It flowers freely after fire.

3 COMMON WOMBAT. One of Australia's many delightful marsupials, the Common Wombat is found in hilly and mountainous country in southern Australia. The wombat has a powerful build, well-suited for digging.

4 MURRAY RIVER, ECHUCA. Rich in history, this town was once an important inland shipping centre, second only to Melbourne, in the days when·riverboats transported wool, wheat and other produce to and from the towns and properties along the Murray, Darling and Murrumbidgee rivers. Today the river traffic is mostly holiday houseboats and paddlesteamers carrying tourists. Echuca is 202 kilometres north of Melbourne.

1 SUNRISE, POWERS LOOKOUT, NEAR WHITFIELD. One of the most rewarding sights in the Australian bush is to see the sun rise over the mountains on a still, summer morning. Powers Lookout is in the north eastern ranges of Victoria. Last century it was used by the notorious bushranger, Harry Power, as a hideout; today, stairs and viewing platforms have been installed in the rocky outcrops near the picnic ground, and stunning views over the King Valley and surrounding ranges can be seen.

2 ALPINE ASH, NEAR HARRIETVILLE. The lovely forests of Alpine Ash trees along the road to Mount Hotham take on a special beauty after a recent fall of snow. Passing through the Bogong National Park, this road leads to the Mount Hotham Ski Resort, and beyond to Omeo. During the ski season, it is compulsory for all motorists on this road to carry snow chains.

1 MELBOURNE AT NIGHT. The capital of Victoria, and Australia's second largest city, the heart of Melbourne is situated around the Yarra River. Trees and lawns grace the banks, and from the walking paths close to the water there are some lovely views of the central city's skyline. It is the only Australian city to have hosted the Olympic Games — and it is probably the only one in the world that declares a Public Holiday to celebrate a horse race.

2 BAKERS GULLY ROAD, BRIGHT. This delightful alpine town is one of the best places in Australia for autumn beauty, and each year many visitors come to see the deciduous trees turn in a blazing kaleidoscope of colour along streets, lanes, in parks and gardens, and by the banks of the Ovens River. Situated 300 kilometres north east of Melbourne, Bright is also the gateway for three ski resorts.

30

QUEENSLAND

The second largest State of the Commonwealth is Queensland which covers an area of more than 1.7 million square kilometres and has a population exceeding 2.3 million. The State is split by the Great Dividing Range, with a lush coastal plain to the east and a larger area of dry plains and plateaux to the west.

The coastline of Queensland was charted, first by James Cook and then by Matthew Flinders, late in the 18th. century. The first European settlement, a penal colony, was established at Moreton Bay in 1824. Later, this colony was moved to the present site of Brisbane. It remained there for 15 years after which free settlement was allowed.

Agriculture is important in Queensland where millions of cattle and sheep graze west of the Great Dividing Range. On the east coast there are thousands of farms which grow sugar cane, pineapples, peanuts and tropical fruits. Major mineral deposits including zinc, silver, lead, bauxite, coal and oil are also found in the State.

Tourism is one of Queensland's major industries. Brisbane, the capital city, lies a few degrees south of the Tropic of Capricorn and is the gateway to instant leisure. Just a short drive to the south are the world-famous resorts of Surfers Paradise and the Gold Coast while to the north is the Sunshine Coast with kilometres of golden sands and surf and seemingly endless sunshine. Further north, just a few hours by air, lies the world's largest coral formations, the Great Barrier Reef. It extends for 2000 kilometres along the coast and is dotted with hundreds of small islands, many of which have been developed as international-standard resorts.

Still further north is one of the world's largest wilderness areas, the Cape York Peninsula. Contrary to popular belief, rain forest covers less than one per cent of this area. Apart from the narrow strip which runs from Cardwell to Cooktown, there are only isolated patches in the north.

NOOSA HEADS, FROM LAGUNA LOOKOUT. This very popular holiday resort lies at the mouth of the beautiful Noosa River, on the coastal area known as the 'Sunshine Coast', in southern Queensland. From the Laguna Lookout, situated in the Noosa National Park, there are wonderful views over the town and surrounding areas. A good car park is provided at the Lookout.

2

1   SUNRISE, PALM COVE. Probably the most
romantic beaches in Australia lie near tropical
Cairns, in the far north of the State. Palm Cove
is about twenty kilometres north of Cairns.

2   SOOTY TERNS, MICHAELMAS CAY. Lying near the
outer Barrier Reef, out from Cairns, this tiny
island is a sanctuary for many birds in the
nesting season.

3   THE GREAT BARRIER REEF, OFF HERON ISLAND. One
of the best places for divers and snorkellers to
see the 'coral gardens' of the Great Barrier Reef
is around Heron Island, lying off the coast at
Gladstone. A great natural wonder of the
world, the 2000 kilometre-long reef is a
complex of innumerable coral reefs, bays,
lagoons, rocky islands, and deep water
channels.

1

2

1 LAKE EACHAM, ATHERTON TABLELAND.
Surrounded by lush tropical rainforest, this
beautiful lake fills the mouth of an old volcano,
and is one of several crater lakes on the
Tableland. Lake Eacham is only 72 kilometres
from Cairns; the nearest town to it on the
Tableland is Yungaburra.

2 PINK ROCK ORCHID. (*Dendrobium kingianum*). This
beautiful orchid is found in south east
Queensland and northern New South Wales,
and favours rocky crevices. It flowers between
August and November.

3 ELEBANA FALLS, LAMINGTON NATIONAL PARK. This
beautiful plateau rising to heights above 1100
metres, lies by the Queensland-New South
Wales border, just behind the Gold Coast, and
is the State's best known national park.
Elebana Falls is only a few kilometres from
O'Reillys Guest House.

1

1 KOALAS, LONE PINE SANCTUARY. An excellent place to see this favourite and endearing Australian native animal is at the Lone Pine Sanctuary in Brisbane. Confined mostly to Victoria, the coastal forests of New South Wales and parts of Queensland, koalas are not so easy to see in their natural habitat. They feed mainly at night, only selecting leaves from about twelve of the 500 odd species of eucalypts.

2 EMU. This tall, flightless bird ranges over mainland Australia, except in dense forests of the east coast. They are renowned for their inquisitiveness — and for their annoying behaviour when tamed as pets.

3 LAWN HILL GORGE NATIONAL PARK. This magnificent gorge lies in remote country north of Camooweal in far western Queensland. Five gorges imprison Lawn Hill Creek, and all are lined with superb tropical vegetation. In the very beautiful second gorge, colourful cliffs rise sheerly from the water up to 60 metres. This photograph shows the second gorge.

2

1

1 BRISBANE. Founded in 1823, Queensland's capital city lies on the Brisbane River, the largest commercial river in Australia, close to the New South Wales border. Just south of the city is a famous wealthy playground: the Gold Coast. The climate is sub-tropical, and in this sunny environment, Brisbane's population enjoys a more relaxed way of life than Australia's southern cities.

2 RAINBOW BEACH, COOLOOLA NATIONAL PARK. Sweeping for many kilometres towards Double Island Point, this magnificent beach is lined with colourful sandstone cliffs — relics of iron-stained dunes that were deposited many thousands of years ago when the sea level was much lower. The small town of Rainbow Beach is 65 kilometres from Gympie.

SOUTH AUSTRALIA

The State of South Australia, with a population of just over 1.3 million occupies about one-fifth of Australia's land mass.

Dutch navigators sailed the waters of South Australia in the 17th. century, but it was not until Colonel William Light arrived in the colony in 1836 that the first permanent settlement was established.

The early years of South Australia were not easy, but by 1844 the colony was producing more than sufficient wheat for its own needs. Major discoveries of copper at Kapunda and Burra added to its growing wealth. Although much of the State is arid, South Australia remains an important wheat growing area and is also Australia's leading producer of grapes for wine and brandy making. The wine industry of South Australia, which owes much of its success to early settlers from Europe, has developed into one of the State's leading tourist attractions, particularly in the Barossa Valley. The State is also an important steel making, engineering and shipbuilding centre, whilst recent discoveries of vast reserves of oil, natural gas, coal and uranium are generating a new era of prosperity.

Adelaide, the capital, is one of the country's most pleasant cities with a well-designed road system, extensive parklands, a background of the Mount Lofty Ranges. It has a wide selection of international class restaurants and the exciting Festival Centre stages the acclaimed Festival of Arts every two years.

Visitors to the State should not fail to visit the magnificent Flinders Ranges — mountains with a robust collection of colourful cliffs, granite peaks, razor-backed ridges and steep gorges. For the more intrepid traveller, the opal mining towns of Andamooka and Coober Pedy offer a faint prospect of instant riches.

1

1 WHITE PAPER DAISIES (*Helipterum floribundum*). After good winter rains, these daisies often carpet the sandy plains of inland Australia.

2 NEAR STURT'S STONY DESERT. In the far north eastern corner of the State, at the edge of Sturt's Stony Desert on Cordillo Downs Station, there are many splendid sand dunes, varying in colour from pale pink to rich red. These dunes stretch far into the desert, breaking the monotony of harsh gibber plains, and continue into the Simpson Desert.

1

1 PURNI BORE, SIMPSON DESERT. At the edge of the desert, near Dalhousie, very hot water from this bore spills along the red sand dunes. The water here is so laden with minerals that colourful deposits have hardened into ridges, shelves, and strange cauliflower formations and patterns around the smaller pools close to the bore head.

2 BUNYEROO VALLEY, FLINDERS RANGES. This beautiful valley is one of many scenic spots lying relatively near the tourist village at Wilpena Pound. In a year of good winter rains, many slopes and river banks are transformed into purple carpets of flowering Salvation Jane. Quorn — the tourist gateway to the Flinders Ranges — lies 324 kilometres north of Adelaide.

3 RIVER GUMS, FLINDERS RANGES. Just south of Wilpena Pound, one of the most scenic roads in this area follows the Moralana Creek, where many magnificent River Gums either line the banks or stand in the usually dry river bed. The River Gum, renowned for its individual grace and character, has a potential life span of well over 500 years.

1

1 THE ADMIRAL ARCH, KANGAROO ISLAND. This dramatic arch is in the cliffs at Flinders Chase, a national park at the south western end of Kangaroo Island. Equally impressive is the huge cave below. Kangaroo Island lies off the Yorke and Fleurieu peninsulas, and is Australia's largest island, after Tasmania.

2 INNES NATIONAL PARK, YORKE PENINSULA. One of the best places to view the spectacular cliffs that lie in this national park at the foot of the Yorke Peninsula, is at Ethel Beach. Embedded in the sand is the wreck of the 'Ethel', which was blown on to the beach during a gale in 1904.

1

1 VICTORIA SQUARE, ADELAIDE. The capital city of South Australia and founded in 1836, Adelaide is situated on a long, narrow plain beside Gulf St. Vincent, and bordered on its eastern side by the picturesque Adelaide Hills. Every two years the city stages what has been recognised as Australia's most important cultural festival, the Festival of Arts.

2 MURRAY RIVER, WALKER FLAT. In many places between Mannum and Renmark the Murray is sheltered by colourful limestone cliffs. From these cliff tops there are splendid views over this great river, now swollen by waters of all its major tributaries. Rising in the Snowy Mountains in New South Wales, the Murray travels 2570 kilometres before flowing into the Southern Ocean at Goolwa — some 170 kilometres on from Walker Flat.

3 COOPER CREEK AT DAWN, NEAR ETADUNNA. The Cooper rises in Queensland, but once it reaches South Australia, it is more often than not a river of sand, with only a few waterholes marking its course.

WESTERN AUSTRALIA

The State of Western Australia is the largest and most sparsely populated in Australia. Covering an area in excess of 2.5 million square kilometres, Western Australia has a population of slightly less than 1.25 million, almost one million of whom live in the capital city, Perth.

European sailors knew of the existence of Western Australia back in the 17th. century but it was not until the 19th. century that James Stirling recommended sites in the Swan River area as being suitable for permanent settlement. The first free-settlers arrived in 1829 with convict labour being used to help establish the new area. Western Australia was granted self-government in 1890, and development of the State accelerated dramatically when the discovery of gold at Coolgardie and Kalgoorlie in the early 1890's brought waves of immigrants westward to cash in on the boom. Since then, Western Australia has developed to the point where it is one of the largest sources of mineral deposits in the world, with enormous mining operations in the Pilbara region of the north west, yielding seemingly endless supplies of iron ore. In addition to iron ore, the State also has significant deposits of diamonds, gold, bauxite and strategic metals such as cobalt, chrome and vanadium.

Perth is often described as the most isolated city in the world with its nearest urban neighbor, Adelaide, some 2700 kilometres away to the east, across the barren Nullabor Plain. This sense of isolation, which may have retarded Perth's growth in earlier years, has nurtured a frontier mentality of independence and self-sufficiency which gives the city its present day vitality. Apart from its enormous mineral wealth, and despite its relatively low rainfall, Western Australia also has a thriving rural industry, particularly in the south-west where wheat and wool are produced in significant quantity.

1

1 SAND GOANNA. Found throughout inland Australia, this large goanna favours raiding rubbish bins in national parks and reserves.

2 JOFFRE GORGE, HAMERSLEY RANGE. This is one of many colourful gorges lying in the Hamersley Range National Park, about 1450 kilometres north of Perth.

FORTESCUE FALLS AND POOL, HAMERSLEY RANGE.
From the cliff-top car park, it is an easy walk
down to this beautiful spot in Dales Gorge.

1

2

1 STIRLING RANGE. Rising abruptly over the plains about 90 kilometres north of Albany in the south west of the State, the Stirling Range is an important national park noted for its profusion of spring wildflowers. There is also a number of challenging hiking tracks that wind up to the range's rugged, stony-faced ridges and peaks.

2 KANGAROO PAW (*Anigozanthos manglesii*). Flowering between August and November, this plant is endemic to Western Australia; it is also the State's floral emblem.

3 KARRI FOREST, NEAR PEMBERTON. In the south west of the State, Warren National Park preserves some of the finest of the accessible virgin karri forest in the area. Within the park runs the Maidenbush Trail, a one-way narrow road that loops through the forest for about seven kilometres. The karri is one of the world's tallest trees.

1

1 BARNETT GORGE, KIMBERLEYS. Lying about four kilometres off the Gibb River Road, this beautiful gorge is one of many found in the wild and remote western Kimberleys. After about two kilometres, the track ends and it is necessary to walk the rest of the distance to the gorge.

2 BOAB AT SUNSET. Growing only in the far north of Australia, these unusual trees with their swollen trunks and ungainly limbs are a distinct feature of the region. They are only in leaf during the Wet Season, at which time exotic, tubular-shaped creamy flowers adorn the trees.

3 GEIKIE GORGE, KIMBERLEYS. Geikie is one of the region's best known scenic attractions, and each year hundreds of visitors come here to take the national park's boat trip through this colourful gorge on the Fitzroy River. Geikie lies sixteen kilometres from the settlement of Fitzroy Crossing.

1 CHEYENS BEACH, DUKE OF ORLEANS BAY. This beautiful beach is part of the coastal wilderness between Cape Arid and Cape Le Grand, east of Esperance on the State's south eastern coast. Off shore lies the Archipelago of the Recherche.

2 PELICANS, AUGUSTA. These pelicans are waiting for fishermen to clean fish at the edge of the Blackwood River, south west Western Australia.

3 MISTY MORNING, NORNALUP INLET. This lovely inlet forms part of the Walpole-Nornalup National Park lying on the south coast 121 kilometres west of Albany. A scenic drive runs through the park, and from a number of vantage points, good views can be seen.

2

1

1 PERTH, FROM KINGS PARK. Capital of Western
Australia, Perth was settled in 1829. The city
lies around the Swan River, which broadens
into the tidal Perth Water before reaching the
Indian Ocean. In the heart of Perth is Kings
Park, where 405 hectares of natural bushland
set on high gound have been preserved.

2 STURT DESERT PEA (Clianthus formosus). This unusual
flower is found throughout the inland from
Western Australia to the plains of New South
Wales, and flourishes in the spring after good
winter rains. Like many Australian
wildflowers, its blooms wilt very quickly after
picking.

2

TASMANIA

The island of Tasmania, which lies across the Bass Strait, about an hour's flying time south of the mainland, has the distinction of being the smallest State in the Commonwealth. The population of almost 500,000 is largely decentralised, with the major concentrations in the Hobart, Launceston, Burnie and Devonport areas.

Tasmania's first European settlement was established in 1804 and for the fifty years that followed, the island served as a penal colony for the British. Much of the State's early history has been preserved and is now a major component in the island's flourishing tourist trade. Among the better-known historic buildings are the ruins of the infamous convict settlement at Port Arthur, which stand as a grim memorial to the 10,000 or more convicts transported from England and held there between 1830 and 1877. Less depressing reminders of Tasmania's past are to be found elsewhere. There are graceful stone bridges, historic buildings painstakingly restored, Australia's oldest theatre and hamlets named after their English counterparts. They have been maintained as if they were transplanted direct from the Old Country.

But despite its fascinating history, Tasmania's main attraction for many people lies in its spectacular scenery, particularly in its national parks and wilderness areas, many of which are yet to be fully explored. Its rugged mountains are studded with lakes, some natural, some made by man as part of the State's hydro-electricity development.

Hiking and bushwalking enthusiasts are amply catered for with guide sheets and information available from the National Parks & Wildlife Service. For those who wish to pursue less physical activities, both Hobart and Launceston offer international standard gambling casinos.

HOBART. This beautiful city set around the broad and deep estuary of the Derwent River is the capital of Tasmania. It is Australia's second oldest city, having been settled in 1804, and fortunately, parts of the city has retained much of its Georgian architecture and historic character.

1

2

1 GUNNS PLAINS. This rich rural area lies in a beautiful valley south of Penguin, on Tasmania's north west coast. An added attraction is the limestone caves, some of which are open to the public.

2 DERWENT RIVER, NEW NORFOLK. One of Tasmania's major rivers, the Derwent is at its most beautiful between Glenora and New Norfolk, in the Derwent Valley. The river rises in Lake St. Clair, and enters the sea downstream from the city of Hobart.

3 RUSSELL FALLS. By far the loveliest in Tasmania, these falls are on the lower slopes of Mount Field, a national park 83 kilometres north west of Hobart. There is an easy ten minute walk to the falls from the car park.

1

1 SUMMIT OF CRADLE MOUNTAIN. From the Face Track on Cradle Mountain, a roughly marked trail over a tangled mass of boulders goes up to the summit and into a Stonehenge-like world of monstrous tors. Although no climbing equipment is needed, this hike is not recommended for the faint-hearted.

2 CRADLE MOUNTAIN. This magnificent mountain of serrated ridgetops and jagged peaks lies in the central Tasmanian highlands, 80 kilometres from Devonport. It is part of a national park that extends as far as Lake St. Clair in the south, the two places being linked by the Overland Track. One of the greatest hazards for hikers in this area is the weather, which can make conditions extremely dangerous.

3 LEATHERWOOD (Eucryphia lucida). This flower is the source of the famous, strong-flavoured honey. Found only in Tasmania in areas of high rainfall, the Leatherwood tree blooms from January to March.

1

1 GORDON RIVER. The tourist launches from Strahan travel 20 kilometres upstream to this point at Butlers Island; from there, the usual mode of transport is by canoe. In 1983 a major victory for conservation was won when plans to dam the river were dropped. The Gordon, and its beautiful tributary the Franklin, are protected by the Wild Rivers National Park.

2 PORT ARTHUR. Built in 1830 and situated on the Tasman Peninsula beyond Eaglehawk Neck, this notorious penitentiary has become a major historic site, attracting thousands of visitors each year. Twenty years after it was abandoned in 1877, a disastrous bushfire swept through the area, destroying many of the buildings.

1

1 NEAR QUEENSTOWN. The extraordinary landscapes around this old mining town in the State's south west, were caused by the early timber-men stripping the hills of trees to feed the furnaces of the copper smelters, which belched sulphur-laden fumes that killed off the remaining vegetation. Many of the colours seen in the ground are the result of mineral leaching.

2 LAKE PEDDER, REFLECTING MOUNT ELIZA. Part of the untamed wilderness of the South West National Park, this man-made lake lies 170 kilometres from Hobart. Although the new lake is beautiful, it was gained only by flooding the original Lake Pedder — a unique natural feature of great significance.

NORTHERN TERRITORY

The Northern Territory covers 1,347,525 square kilometres and is a land of unique contrasts and spectacular scenery.

The home of aboriginal tribes for countless thousands of years, the Territory was first charted by Dutch navigators in the 17th. century, but no permanent settlement was established until 1824. During its early days, development of the Territory was slow but the discovery of gold in 1863 significantly accelerated its growth. At that time the Northern Territory came under the control of the State of South Australia, with the Federal Government assuming administrative control in 1911. In 1978 the Territory was granted self-government, but despite the development of extensive mineral resources, much of the Territory remains as it has always been — a land of endless horizons, vast deserts, tropical vegetation and rugged mountain ranges where a sense of timelessness is found.

Darwin, the administrative centre and main port located on the north-western coast, was all but wiped off the map by a cyclone in 1974. Much has now been rebuilt, but to many residents the cruel scars left by Cyclone Tracy will never fully heal.

The only other town of any size is Alice Springs, a major tourist centre and the jumping-off point for some of the Territory's most famous attractions including Ayers Rock, the Olgas, Kings Canyon, Ormiston Gorge and Simpson Gap. Further north, the Top End, as it is known, is a wildlife paradise with buffalo, crocodiles, wallabies, kangaroos, wild pigs and a dazzling array of birdlife.

Perhaps in no other area of the continent is the European visitor so conscious of the Dreamtime — the spiritual heritage of the Australian Aborigine. The Northern Territory is home for almost half the country's Aboriginal population. It is also rich in rock carvings said to be over 30,000 years old — testimony to suggestions that the Australian Aborigine belongs to the world's longest surviving civilisation.

1 STURT'S DESERT ROSE *(Gossypium sturtianum)*. This shrub of inland Australia flowers between June and November. It is the floral emblem of the Northern Territory.

2 KINGS CANYON. This incredible canyon lies in the George Gill Range, 370 kilometres south west of Alice Springs, near Wallara Ranch. To see it properly it is necessary to walk to the top and along the plateau to the head of the canyon. This is from the Garden of Eden, a narrow gorge at the head of the canyon.

SUNSET, AYERS ROCK. This magnificent sandstone monolith is the earth's greatest slab of exposed rock, with a height of 348 metres and a circumference of 9.5 kilometres. Lying in the Uluru National Park, 426 kilometres south west of Alice Springs, this renowned tourist attraction is also a ritual ground of sacred Dreamtime legends and myths for the Aborigines.

1

1 TREPHINA GORGE. Situated 76 kilometres east of Alice Springs and near the Ross River Tourist Resort, this gorge is at its best when the craggy red walls are mirrored in still water. Most times there is a pool in the gorge, left from Trephina Creek's last flood.

2 ABORIGINAL ROCK PAINTINGS, KAKADU NATIONAL PARK. These motifs are among many paintings on a cave wall near the Nourlangie Waterhole.

1

1 KATHERINE GORGE. A national park, Katherine Gorge lies near the town of Katherine, 322 kilometres south of Darwin. For about twelve kilometres from the ranger's jetty, thirteen spectacular gorges line the Katherine River. Boat trips run regularly into the gorges; they can also be seen from the walking path that meanders along the cliff tops.

2 SUNSET, KAKADU NATIONAL PARK. At Cooinda, the Jim Jim Creek spills into Yellow Water Lagoon, which is part of Kakadu, situated at the edge of Arnhem Land, east of Darwin. Dramatic sunsets are frequently seen over this lagoon from the nearby camping ground.

3 WATERFALL CREEK. Also known as the U.D.P. Falls, this lovely nature reserve is situated about 100 kilometres north east of Pine Creek. From the camping ground it is possible to climb to the top of the waterfall, which drops to this beautiful pool.

TWIN GHOST GUMS, NEAR ALICE SPRINGS. On very
cold winter mornings, sometimes mist still
clings to the ground as the sun rises to light
the Razorback Range, behind these two lovely
gums. Standing close to the main road west of
Alice Springs, the trees are easily viewed by
motorists.

THE OLGAS. Lying 32 kilometres west of Ayers Rock in Uluru National Park, this unique group of standstone monoliths rise almost in a circle from the surrounding plain to form one of the world's most fascinating sights. The highest of the 30 odd domes is Mt. Olga, at 540 metres.

1   SALTWATER CROCODILE, ADELAIDE RIVER. This dangerous reptile inhabits estuaries, rivers and lagoons of far northern Australia. Protected by law in 1971 when hunters had reduced its numbers to alarmingly low levels, the 'salty' as it is popularly called, is now on the increase. Tourists are wise to heed the notices warning against swimming that are being placed in many spots in the north!

2   MINURIA (*Minuria leptophylla*). Favouring sandy soils of the inland, this attractive daisy flowers between July and November.

3   CANNON HILL, ARNHEM LAND. Although included in the Kakadu National Park, Cannon Hill is part of the restricted Arnhem Land Reserve. This is Red Lily Lagoon at the edge of the Arnhem Land Escarpment, and has been named for the lovely Lotus Lilies that grow profusely here.

THE SMITH STREET MALL, DARWIN. Capital of the Northern Territory, and Asia's gateway to Australia, the tropical city of Darwin celebrated its centenary in 1969. Five years later the city was virtually rebuilt after the devastation caused by Cyclone Tracy.